The 24 Hour Store
was
Closed

by

Paul Richmond

Dedicated to everyone who was

true to themselves.

Doesn't mean I liked who you are.

Published by Human Error Publishing
www.humanerrorpublishing.com
paul@humanerrorpublishing.com

Copyright © 2020
by
Human Error Publishing & Paul Richmond

ISBN: 978-1-948521-01-7

Front Cover: A 24 hr store in Buffalo, New York
Paul Richmond

Back Cover Photo - Paul Richmond

How To Find

A Bell

1)

On seeing what looks like a small bell
Sitting on a table
You remember
A bookstore
Cafe
A small bell above the door
That rang each time the door
Was opened or closed
You were there
With your love
They bought you a book
You ate yummy deserts
Drank
Lots of coffee
The book
Sits on a shelf
Never read
Many years later
It is just you and the book

2)

A bell from a clown's hat
Was found
In the hay
In the cage
That was center stage
Where the lion's performed

This clown had dreamt
Of being in the lion's cage
Performing with the lions

It was late at night
The lion's performing cage was empty
Everyone had gone to sleep
Including the lions
The clown entered
Hearing the cheering crowds
The roar of the lions
Started to perform

The clown was yelling commands
For the cheering crowds
Which woke the lions
Being hungry and restless
They went to investigate

The police asked many questions
Why on this particular night
That the clown went into the cage
The lions had not been fed
The drunk lion keeper
Had not closed the gate
Between the lion's cages
And the large performing cage
What happen to the clown
Where were the lions

The clown was never seen again
Either were the lions
The door to the performance cage
Was open
There was no sign
Of what happened
Besides one of the clown's
Bells
Was found in the hay

3)

It looks like a little bell
Actually a valuable part
In a mechanical device
That breaks
There in a large box
Must be hundreds of them
Found at a tag sale
On a table with a sign
Three cents each
Only having ten dollars
You want all of them
You consider grabbing the box
And running
You decide instead to
Muster your best
I am paying too much
But hey I'll give you ten dollars
For all of them
The ten dollars is snatched
Out of your hand
In case you might change your mind
You pick up the large box
You know that they are selling
On E Bay for $36 each
You keep up the act
I don't know why I bought these
You walk off
With dreams of being rich

The son who was manning the table
Said Pa
What is he going to do with those
Hell if I know
Put out another box
Don't put so many in this time

4)

I became hypnotized
The one year old
Just held the tiny bell
In their hand
The parents yelled at me later
They could of choked on it
They put everything in their mouth
You don't give a one-year old small items
To play with
It was a small bell
Being held with tiny fingers
Eyes wide open
Staring at what was between
Their fingers
Turning there head
This way and that
Every so often
The amazement
Watching
I told myself
I need to be reminded
Of the amazement

Street Dog

I was sitting
Eating a hamburger
In the park
When a street dog approached growling
Looking really mean
I could see he or she was scared
Hungry
I broke off a quarter of my hamburger
And threw it in their direction
The street dog stopped growling
Looked at me
Looked at the hamburger
Said Thanks
But I need more then this
Then they swallowed down the hamburger
Looking up
I threw them another piece
They swallowed it down
They looked really thin
I took a bite and threw them the rest
They swallowed it
Then came towards me
Looking like they wanted to be petted
As street dog got closer
I reached out my hand
And they bit me
I scream
And yelled
What the hell did you do that for
I just gave you my food
The street dog
Said
One act of kindness
Doesn't wipe away

All the
Pain,
Anger
and
Suffering
I am sorry

Sunday School Teacher - True Story

He lived in one of the hill towns
In the house his Grandfather's
Grandfather built
He was born there
He never went to church
Yet he taught Sunday School
In the basement of the Church
This went on for many many years
Then a new priest took over
He met with the Sunday School teacher
And said that he would have to go to church
If he was going to teach Sunday School
The priest wanted him to come to church
And sing the hymns
It turned into a big argument
The Sunday school teacher
Just told the priest flat out
There was no way he was going to church
And he wasn't going to sing any hymns
The reason he gave
He knew that if he were to go to church
And sing the hymns
He would die
No church for him
The Sunday School teacher continued to teach
The priest learned that it was his birthday
At the Sunday mass
He asked that someone go down and get the Sunday
school teacher
So that they could sing happy birthday
When he came up
The priest handed him the book of hymns
And asked him to sing along
He sang three verses

Then he fell to the ground dead
The priest was transferred to another church
Where he insisted everyone
Go to church

Are You Listening

In the land of Silence
The fear of words
Keeps control in power

If you listen closely
You'll hear whispers
Traveling on the wind

When control worries
The volume on Noise
Is turned up
Making it harder to hear
The whispers
Breaking the silence

In the land of Silence
The whispers can't be stopped
Going over walls
Through barbwire
Some say they come
From the forbidden zones

Robot cops are sent in
But it's too late
The whispers are getting louder
I am listening

This was logged in a journal in the past
About the future
Which is now the present
Which the panelists are arguing
Is this Sic-Fi or reality

Where Do Victims Come From

As the camera zooms in
We are getting a closer look
At
The flood victims
The hurricane victims
The war victims
The torture victims
The victims of terrorism
The victims of corporations
The victims in the camps
We are all victims
Of all the traumas
Clinging to this small rock
Floating through space

Where we create victims

When They Kick In The Doors

When the uniforms
Come rushing in
After kicking in the doors

They don't care
That you are a vegetarian, vegan, breatharian
Or that you are an urban hunter
Only eating local squirrel, apartment rats, and alley dogs
They don't care

They don't care if you eat pussy
Or like to suck cock
Or both
Or
You have a spear, wear a tutu with flippers on your head
Because your lover likes it
When you're wild and crazy
They really don't care

When the uniforms
Come rushing in
After kicking in the doors

They don't care
That you will only eat
Organic ice cream made with
GMO free organic local dairy milk
Made with local organic raspberries
Picked by people who love raspberries
They don't care

When the uniforms kick in the doors
They are rushing in
To get all of us
It's not going to be a party

There is a Howling

When the food arrives
Top Dog
Eats first

There have been
Bloody
Discussions
Understandings
That when the food arrives
Top Dog eats first

A whisper is heard
Among those waiting their turn
There are more of us
We need to fight
Top Dog
Collectively
Top Dog
Will step aside
Then we all eat

Out of the silence
There comes a howling
Top Dog
Takes notice
With his mouth full
He steps aside
Acting like he was done
This is the moment
When everyone moves in
The scent
Of scarcity
Brings on fear
The bloody discussions

Begin again
Will we end up
With a new Top Dog

Heard above the yelps
There is a Howling

Shooting Stars

Everyone searches
For the darkest places
In the hopes to see
The most shooting stars

He prefers
To watch for them
In the day light

He sees more shooting stars
Then 10 of them put together
And it irks them
That he doesn't even care

What put them over the edge
Was the smirk
When he told them
He does it with his eyes closed

Lunch

A bartender
Who had two elderly parents
Helped seniors raise money
By selling their raffle tickets
To the bar patrons

He waited
Until they had at least two drinks
Then he would give his pitch
He sold a lot of raffles

Raising the money
The seniors needed
To have lunch

An Artist Statement

When an Artist turned on the water faucet
Wanting a fresh clear glass of water
Only to hear a gas being released
Inspired, lit a match
They always wanted a blow torch
They had collected hundreds of
Discarded cell phones
They started melting them together
Into a large sculpture
When it was done
They struggled to name it
"We hate the environment"
"We've poisoned everything"
"We are all refugees"

A gallery agreed to show the work
On one condition
The name is changed
The Gallery called it
"We are all connected"
The Gallery owner said
This would go over much better
With the gallery"s clientele
Who were looking for escapism art

It sold
The Gallery wanted
The artist to make 10 more
This could be the start of something big
It was
The whole neighborhood
Blew sky high
The explosion
Rattled windows

20 miles away
The guy who sold the town on fracking
Was never seen again
The price of the sculpture
Jumped a hundred times
At the auction of dead artists
A group protested out side the event
Demanding the sculpture be renamed
We are all fucked

Wheel Wall

(This was read at an "Arts in the Orchard" event, where
several poets, dancers, singers did pieces in front of
various art installations scattered in the orchard, mine
was 8 larger steel wagon looking like wheels, welded
together to make a wall)

Wheel Wall
Is made of Steel and Paint

The Wall that is being built
Along the Southern border
Is made of Steel and Paint

Wheel Wall
Was put here in the orchard
No Trees were cut down

Building the Wall
At the Rio Grande
There were 29 laws protecting
The 17 miles of trees, wet lands
Yet the wall is being built at this moment
Total destruction
Every tree, wet lands.....
Total destruction
Yes the Orange one
Is building walls
What is being done
Is not making us Great
Tear down the Walls
That keep you in
Tear down the
Walls
That keep others out

Gives us the
Wheel Wall
Walls that you can see through
You can pass through
Walls that are called art
Walls built from reclaimed material
Matt Johnson the artist
Felt his sculpture was like a drawing

My first thought was
Giant Wagon Wheels
Those who went west
In the hope to find
A new life
We are all refugees

Bill

Was a writer
A military man
His writings all started with
A woman I almost knew

A woman I almost knew 234
He had met her
On this island
On that island
He had gone to West Point
He started to ask questions
He had a sense that something
Was wrong
With what he was involved in
Viet Nam in the 70's

In the late 90's
He stood on the town common
With the peaceniks
Those against the present wars
He was always there
With his dog
He held hand made signs
Where he had scribbled his thoughts
He was well read
He had lived it first hand
He was also a poet
He started to come to the monthly readings
When you spend time with people
You build relationships

He had a stroke
His dog died

He was committed to rehab
It didn't look like he was going to get out
I was told his brother died
Another poet went to visit
Told everyone he was gone
No info on where he went

One day driving in town
I saw him walking with a woman
I was positive
I tried to turn around
Couldn't
When I finally did
He was no where to be found
I was told he had never recovered from his stroke
Never regained the use of his arm or leg
He was suddenly gone

I have a pretty good idea what happened to him
I saw him walking in the streets
Talking
Laughing
With a woman
He almost knew
235

The Rock Guy

A lot of cars going by
Car after car after car
And he's standing
on the other side
of the highway
The cars are going by him
So many lanes on each side
Looking at the other side
With no way
To get to the other side

There are others standing around
Gazing at the other side

He finds himself
Walking along the highway
Looking, thinking about the other side
As he's walking
He sees it
In the ditch
A large rock
This is what he needs
He starts to walk towards
The first lane
With the Rock
Above his head
Like he is going to throw it
And the car stops
He steps into the next lane
Lane after lane
The cars stop
A crowd is forming
Cheering him on
Is he going to make it

He gets to the other side
He does a little dance
And he heads back across
When he gets to the other side
He tells the crowd
For a small fee
He'll take them across
As he starts to take people across
His business starts
He has dreams
He could train people to do this
Have a company with company T-shirts
With a rock on it
He's dreaming big
Then the police arrived

He was famous
For a short period of time
The paper did a story on him
Everyone was talking about it
The rock guy
He tried to sell rocks to tourists

He ended back at the intersection
With his old sign
He was a homeless Vet
He'd work for food
He's the rock guy
He's the rock guy
Do you want to buy a rock
He's got one for you
He's the rock guy

Wild Parties At the Senior Home

Word was passed
From room to room
By Mable
Who for hours
Roams the halls
Some say looking for a way out

Beth made up
All the name tags
Drawing on each
To give each name a little flare

Billy had saved up all the crackers
That came with his soup
Hoping someone was taking care
Of the cheese

It had been decided
By those who could
Still think of such things

Jean would give the signal
Right after morning singing
We would all refuse to go back
To our rooms
No nap today
Today we were going to party down

It was written in the staff log
Jean yelled PARTY
And all hell broke loose
Janet handed out the name tags
Randomly
So Leona was Stanley

And Dave was Roxie
Singing broke out
Though it was hard to tell
Since they were all singing
A different song

They went up to each other
And called out the name
On the name tag
And laughed so hard
That they pissed and shit
In their pants
Which wasn't that unusual

Some staff members joined in
Laughing hysterically
The up roar of partying
Was brought
To a silence
When Linda's loud voice
Cried out
But I am Doug
I always wanted to be Doug
Please let me be Doug

Linda had started chanting
I am Doug I am Doug
Which started everyone chanting
Screaming out

I am a dancer
I wanted children
I wanted to travel
I am an artist

It took hours
Actually most of the next week

For the staff
To calm everyone down

In Large letters it was stated in the log
There was to be no more parties

This wasn't the purpose of the facility
They weren't set up to handle
People coming to grips
With their lives
What they've done
And not done
Had they been true to themselves

The staff was told
Stick to bingo
Tossing the big ball
Stop any activities
Where residents
Think about their lives
Realize they are running out of time
It could lead to mayhem

Not The Good Guys

I grew up in Buffalo, New York
Watching football
On Sunday afternoons
With World War ll veterans
My uncles drinking beer
On the nightly news
We watched civil rights activists
Being attacked by dogs
Beaten with fire hoses
We watched parades of
Coffins and coffins of dead solders
From the far off jungles of Vietnam

I was told
Americans are the good guys
The cowboys with white hats
The gunslinger killing all the bad guys
We were protecting the world
From Socialism, Communism
And Fascism
We were defending capitalism and democracy
As if they were one and the same

I was told
We were the melting pot of the world
Where everyone wanted to come to be free
The Statue of Liberty
Standing tall in the harbor
With its lamp held high
The writing on the tablets
Welcoming the tired and poor
The huddled masses
Wanting to breathe free
Offering the homeless shelter

Welcoming them to the land of plenty
There is plenty for the 1%
The homeless and the poor
Fight for crumbs
All resources funding endless wars
Based on lies
America has become a land of private prisons
Secret prisons
Water boarding and torture
What happened to the good guys
We watch children put into cages
Separating immigrant families never to be reunited
Our history classes never focused on
The broken treaties,
Genocide home and abroad
Slavery,
Crushing worker's rights
Women's rights
Our moral compass of racism
The environmental destruction
Destroying democracies
Installing dictators
The real history
So many lies

Where are the good guys
I was told
I believed
I was told
I believed
Then I learned the truth
Now it's time
To stop the lies
To make good on the promises

The Three "Rs"
Reading, 'Riting and 'Rithmetic

(Whisper) Shhhhhh
Everyone get in line
Quiet
Follow me
We need to hide
In the closet
Close the door
Close the door

(Gun Shots Heard)

I know what's wrong with the schools
We need to get back to the basics
You remember the 3 R's don't ya
reading
riting
rithmetic

The 3 R's
Except
riting – spelled with an w
rithmetic spelled with an a
I think we have been lied to
I think it's all failed
It's not because of the spelling

It's time for a new schoolhouse

Yeah
When I went to school
We walked 100's of miles
Through 100's of feet of snow
As the story goes

I learned how to
Duck and Cover

We practiced diving under our desks
Kneeling in the hallway
Facing the wall
Heads to the ground
Our hands
Behind our necks
No giggling
This is serious
Taking Cover
We were told
Duck and cover
Would protect us
From the Nuclear incineration

But there is no protection

There was no protection
From the bullies either
The adults didn't stop them
From beating us up in the hallway and on the playground

Now my grand kids
Duck and cover
Dive under their desks
Hide in closets
School shootings
Just another beautiful day in the neighborhood

Students asking for safety and an education
Instead of
Building bullet proof rooms
Paying armed guards
Selling guns to all the teachers

Where's the money for
The teachers
For mentoring
Students aren't numbers
Filling in boxes on tests
Enslaved in debt for a useless degree

What happened to life skills
What happened to the joy of learning

Give me some real R's
The ability to reason
Some R e s p e c t Respect
Relationships
With each other
Our environment

Our Responsibilities
For future generations
It's time to stop the lies

Fund the schools
Not the military
Put an end to
Duck and Cover
Never again
Never again

Throw Sand

This comes from the great epic
A memoir
A drama
Of how I survived
The sand box

One incident
Involved my toy trucks
As weapons
Taken from me
And used to hit me

I did learn early on
I could throw sand
It deters them for a short period of time
It usually brings retaliation
It doesn't have a long lasting effect

I am not going to give away
All my secrets of how I survived the sandbox
It seems I still need them

My Darling

What's Blowing in the wind
Is death Radiation
Stagnation
Racial discrimination
Separate nations
Humiliations
Castrations
Dead Fish animations
Sexual stimulations
Small Farm Elations
Saving the river jubilations
An afternoon lover's intoxications
We grow inspirations
The microphone's screaming agitations
While you are my delectation

Plan B

As I approach the table
They sense I am coming
Their instinct is to stop moving
They hold completely still
No movement
Without any movement
There is a chance
That I don't see them

I see them
They try and make a run for it
These guys are lucky
I just sweep them to the floor
With my hand
It depends on how many
How many times they are in my space
If the sink is filled
I have flushed them down the drain
Wondering if the ones who escaped
Pass the word
We might want to try somewhere else
Or just avoid the sink

Extra Cheese

Hello
Welcome to customer support
Before we get started
I need to know
Are you at
46th and 8th street

I don't know I am visiting
Hey where are we
40th and what and 7th
8th
Yeah we're at 48 and 8th

46 and 8th

Yeah that's it

It looks
Like you are on the third floor
You're in the back room
Is that correct

Wow you guys are amazing
Listen
I have been on hold for over 8 hours
This is important to me
You guys say you want to hear from us
I love you guys
You have to correct this
Make sure it doesn't happen again
You almost lost
One of your faithful
I am just hoping this was a fluke
Just a bad employee

It's what I look forward to everyday
That all sounds great sir
Which product are we talking about

Yummie a gogo
With extra cheese

Yes that is one of our favorite products

Exactly and during these times
Of mass depression
Everything going to Hell
Knowing
A Yummie a gogo with extra cheese
Would always be there
Makes life worth living

That's our goal sir
So what went wrong

When I got home
With my Yummie a gogo
You can't imagine
The rage
The disappointment
The sense of being ripped off
Once again
Why me
I was about to commit suicide
When suddenly I felt I can't give up
We must save the Yummie a gogo
With extra cheese

Ok what is it
What was wrong sir

It didn't have extra cheese

What

I ordered extra cheese
There's no reason to get a
Yummie a gogo
Unless you are going to have Extra Cheese on it
It didn't
Come with the extra cheese

How do you know

It's obvious
I have eaten thousands of these
I know what it looks like
To have extra cheese
This was scary
Was this the beginning of a cheese scarcity

Sir I am with you on this
It makes me ill to even
Think of a
Yummie a gogo
Not having extra cheese
I am so sorry
I am sending you
Ten coupons for free
Yummie a gogo's with extra extra cheese
We take care of our family around here

Thanks so much
That makes me feel great
Hanging up
My eye caught
The cold Yummie a gogo
with No extra cheese
Sitting on the table
The more I stared at it

I got more and more riled up
I realized I wasn't done discharging
So I called again
No extra cheese
Is just not acceptable

Pick Up Dinner

A group of turkeys
Walk through our yard
They keep coming back
I say to an old timer
I think about having one for dinner

He says of course
We ate them all the time
I said did you shoot them

He said no

Did you catch them with a net

He said no

How did you do it

We feed them Rum soaked raisins
They loved them
They always came back

There was always one of them
Who ate too many
Rum soaked raisins

Who would stumble
Fall to the ground
We'd go over
And pick up dinner

Eyes

Why are you staring
So intently
Into my eyes

I can tell you
There's no need to waste your time
You're not going to find
What you are looking for
In these eyes

I am not the cure for your loneliness
So stop staring
Nothing is going to change
I know you believe if you look
Long enough
You will see what you want to see

How long will you look
Will you finally see
You're not going to find
What you are looking for
In these eyes

I Wondered How Good She Is

We are sitting in a park
Talking
She was laid off
She was asking
What am I to do
Her view on life
Boiled down
To two options
I am only good at sucking cock
Or shoveling shit
She kept saying it
Over and over again
I am only good at sucking cock
Or shoveling shit
For some reason
Every time she said it
I couldn't think of anything else
How good was she
At shoveling shit
I hated shoveling shit

The Past

I can tell you about my past
What I experienced
Living in Buffalo, NY
A steel town

Those who lived near the plant
Had a black film
On the outside and the inside
Of their houses
Clothes hung out on the line
Catching the wind to dry
Turned black

The lake caught on fire

Whole neighborhoods were built on Love Canal
A chemical waste dump
Birth defects
Mothers fought and organized
Won
Lost loved ones

Open Nuclear Waste pits
Given to the town West Valley
The town was given a new school
Lights for the new streets
And birth defects

There were battles with the police
In the hopes to save a park
That became a parking lot

In high school we were stopped
From swimming in Lake Erie

Strange rashes
Fish with open soars
Were not eaten by the rich
Some questioned the chemical dumps
The open Nuclear pits

Elm disease
Taught me the name of the trees
That disappeared
Had us looking at the sky
Suddenly we were exposed
The canopies were gone
Everything was bare

I don't live there anymore
Most of my family has died
I visit rarely
I try not to visit the past

The Evidence

His grandfather's grandfather
Owned a fishing boat
Took people out fishing
When they caught fish
They would pose
In front of his sign
On the dock

Over the years
Hundreds of photos
Were taken
The grandson found
The box of the photos
The fish got smaller over the years
It was very noticeable
The fish were disappearing

The Endless Nightmare

The first time
It's hard to believe

The second time
There must be a misunderstanding

The Third time
You realize it's deliberate

Once you've lost count
You know it's a nightmare

You try to wake up

You think surely
It will become obvious
The vehicle is out of control
You're hoping the screaming
Will wake everyone up

Instead
Everything keeps going on
As if there is nothing wrong

Can no one see
This beautiful world
Being destroyed
The cutting of trees
The dumping of poisons
Into the water
The killings
The bombings
Children in cages

The weapons of mass destruction
From military exploits based on lies
Are slowly killing everything
As the massive waste sites are leaking

The making of endless waste
We can't get rid of
We will soon be drowning in it
Why isn't it obvious
And when it is
Why are we so helpless
In stopping it
Changing it
Told we can't

We can
We have to believe our showing up matters
Yes we can shut the place down
No one believes it
So it isn't done
It is happening in other parts of the world
In France
It can be done
For future generations

Listen

She woke up
With the voice of her father
Calling her

He is dead
She often hears his voice
This was different
There was an urgency

She tried to go about her day
Her father's voice
Grew louder and louder

She told a friend
Accustomed to these experiences
Her friend suggested
She go to the grave

As she drove to the grave
Her father was yelling
On arrival
She found
Her brother
Digging up the grave

He hated that his father
Was buried in Belgium
He wanted him to be buried
In Germany
She had honored
Her father's wishes
Burying him in Belgium

The police were called

The brother finally stopped
The grave was filled back in
Her father was silent
She was reminded
To listen

Which Side Of The Fence

It was reported
That someone was climbing the fence
Men in uniforms were called in
When they got there
The person had climbed down

The men in uniforms
Stood
On a hill
Located on the other side
Of this very high fence
Looking down on the group of people
Who had gathered on the other side

On seeing the officers
They started to throw rocks
The fence being high
The uniforms a good distance away
The rocks fell short

It was disputed whether or not
The young man that was shot
10 times
Had thrown any rocks or climbed the fence
Or was just one of the people walking by

The American officer shot
10 times
Only stopping
To reload

His defense
He felt his life was threatened
As he stood a good distance away

On top of a hill
Behind a tall fence

The young man
A Mexican
Lying dead in Mexico

An American in uniform
Standing in America
No charges were filed

I Have Business To Take Care Of

A cousin stopped by
He said he had a dream
His father came to visit

His father has been dead for years
My father took care of his father
Had bought him a pair of new shoes
Took him to his company's picnics
Was like a father to him
His father had gone to the store
Was never seen again

My cousin said
His father walked into his bedroom
Woke him with his entrance
Dropping bags to the floor
My cousin asked what was he doing here
He said he had some business to take care of
My cousin started to talk to his dad
About the business he had inherited from him
How well it was doing
That he would be proud
His father said he was proud
Didn't have time to talk
He had some business to take care of
And left

My cousin came the next day
To tell my brother the dream
He said it felt strange
My brother told him
My dad died last night

Once Upon A Time

The question is
Is this a true story
I can tell you what is true
I had long hair and still do
I owned a pair of white earth shoes
I went out west several times
Hitchhiked
Took buses
Drove In vehicles that over heated
I was a juggler
I knew many people
Who had to hide their sexuality
A white supremacist said he wanted to kill me
I had many girl friends
Who weren't interested in me
I was asked
How many times
Was I going to squeeze those babies

With that in mind
This is the story

She said
I am feeling desperate
And looking at you
I realized how desperate I am

It's these types of experiences
That can damage you
Emotionally
For life

Luckily
I was given

The vaccine
At an early age

She explained
She needed me to
Go to a family gathering out West
We were to act like
We were two heterosexuals madly in love
On seeing this
Her family who were rich
Would give her money

The family event was 3 days long
I would be staying at a fancy resort
All the food and drinks I could consume
We would share a room
I could fondle all I wanted
At given time periods
No intercourse

Since I was on the road
And eating had been slim
And I was ready to fondle
I was in love

This was 1970
She had no interest in men
Didn't want to explain her sexuality
To her family
She didn't want to go alone
And have to endure family friends
Wanting to matchmake
A cousin, such a nice boy
Who later they realized had no interest in girls

As she looked me over
She said her father will probably

Want to pay me to disappear
I would get a percentage of the money
Depending on my bargaining skills
Other wise she would get the money
I would get bus fare

We had to travel to California
In a Opel Kadett
That could only go 45 top speed
And then over heat

This gave us more then enough time
To really test our acting skills
Of being two lovers madly in love
During these rehearsals
She tried to kill me
Once in Nebraska at an abandoned campground
Once in the desert
After running out of gas
Once in the parking lot of the resort

Luckily a cousin arrived
As she had me on the hood
Of the car
Strangling me

When they looked at us strangely
She smiled
And said he likes it rough

Her father did hint of money immediately
Her sister was giving me the eye
But there was no interest there
The family was willing to have
Anyone take her away
There was a brother
He was a white supremacist

Always giving me the finger
And mouthing from across the room
You are dead

On the first night
I obviously had too much to drink
I tried to juggle
Some home made flaming torches
Luckily the fast response
Of the staff
Quickly put out the fire
Saving part of the tent

Fondling was suppose to be
A part of the deal
But after a short time
She said to me
I had to let go of her breast
She couldn't believe anyone
Would want to squeeze
Those babies that much

I was offered the money
Before the morning of the second day
I negotiated
A few drinks for the road
I was given bus fare
Her uncle being a cop
Made it clear I wanted to get on the bus

On getting on the bus
As the story goes
The only open seat
Was next to a women
Who asked if she could pay me
To not sit there
After the 11 hour bus ride
We were together for a few months

Do you have the time

Oh no I am late again
Will it be different with bitcoins

I am asking do you have the time

Where would I have put it

Don't you have a clock on the wall

Is that where it lives

I don't have time to answer these questions
I have a schedule

I guess I wasn't invited
Don't know anything about schedules
Places to be

Well what do you do with your time
When you find where you hide it
For safe keepings

That is the question
What does one do
When one finds their time

Silence for dramatic effect
Some call it art
Some hope it changes the world

Back to the question
Do you have the time

She was behind the counter

I needed to know
What time it was
There were no clocks on the walls
My cell phone had a dead battery
I walked up
She was pretty busy
People in line
She saw me
Smiled
It was my turn
I asked
Do you have the time?
She answered
When do you want me

Snap Fiction and Poetry

I took part in an event
Where writers
Dug through hundreds of photos
Family photos
10 different families
All mixed together
With the only hint
Some times written on the back
Of the photo
A name.
As one of the writers
I was to find a number of photos
Using them as prompts

The Photos I found and incorporated into a story were;

1) You are only looking at the back of the legs of three women standing. Two are wearing white socks, the other woman is wearing black socks

2) Looking at a woman's breast in a low cut gown

3) A Dog sitting in the yard called Jasper

4) A pool with people around it and a man in the pool dunking a child called Baptism

5) A family in the front yard, the father throwing a baby in the air

6) A women with her back to the camera wearing a big hat

7) A series of pictures of three men standing together, all

different men in each picture, the names were written on the back, each series has one of the men identified as Dick

8) Three men are in the picture one on a motor bike the other two men standing next to the bike in woods

What I wrote

This story is obviously about the past
Since we don't take pictures of the future
It is also about healing
First let me set one thing straight
my name is Richard, not Dick

As a child I had no memory of my father
throwing me into the air.
Probably due to the number of times he didn't catch me
It only came up later in therapy
Why I had a fear of flying

Next I want to talk about our dog Jasper
He looked so cute in the picture
The shelter hadn't told us he was a fugitive from 4 states
for bitting children
He eats anything smaller than him
He was trained as a CIA attack dog
I will never forget that first night
My parents left me and Jasper
Alone in my bedroom
So we could get acquainted
I jumped from the second floor window
Probably another reason for my fear of flying

As a kid I didn't have many friends
So I was thrilled when Billie invited me over to his house
to swim in his pool
Once In the water

I was told I was being baptized
I realized later this is where I got my fear of someone
trying to drown me

As a young man I bought a motor bike
My mother thought it was because
I love to ride in the country far away from people
This police photo of me on the motor bike
And the two guys dealing contraband
Exposed the truth

From an early age Aunt Mabel
Would always come up to me
Bend forward with her breasts in my face
Then ask me what color are my eyes
This became an on going sore spot
With future lovers
I never knew what color their eyes were

My first girl friend was the one wearing the black socks
Everyone wore white socks
On seeing those black socks
I was sure she was the one for me

But then I met the woman with the hat
I loved that hat
I had 3 other lovers who wore the same hat
Finally I just bought the hat
And saved everyone a lot of pain

In my healing work
I have created a little alter
Where I sit in front of the pair of black socks
And the hat
And Jasper's head that I had mounted and stuffed
And I do my daily mantra
My name is Richard
I am not a Dick

What is the Plan

When the camera zooms in
A Politician
is being interviewed
About the gathering
In the center of town
With all the loud drumming
Late into the night
People dancing around the bonfire
Naked
The Politician was asked
Do they have a plan

When the camera zooms in
We do see people naked
We hear loud drumming
Some say they are dancing
To an untrained eye
It looks like people
Jumping around
Naked
To the beat of the drums

The politician was asked
Do your constituents of naked people
Have anything to offer
Besides the present situation is looking doomed

The politician said
There was talk of a plan
There were meetings
A vision
Of what could be
What steps were needed
To make it happen

Now was the hard part
Making it happen
How to bring people together
To make it happen

It was suggested that
Possibly dancing naked
Around a fire
To loud drumming
Was not for everyone
One of the naked people
Was interviewed
Asked would the group be willing to compromise
Putting on some clothes
If that would bring more people to their fire
Would they do it
The naked person stated
There were arguments
Between those who wanted to stay pure
And those that wanted to reach out to more people
Some argued once they agreed to put clothes on
It wouldn't stop there
As the arguments continued
The drumming got louder

The politician ended the interview
By saying
This is a small group
Until more join the circle
Or they pay me more money
I have nothing further to say

The police will be sent in
For they are disturbing the peace

When the police showed up
Everyone agreed
They needed a plan

You Score

Just think
It seems unimaginable
That you would be able
To just walk right in
There were no lines to get into
You didn't have to camp out
You didn't have to fight your way
Through the stampede
Fearing that you might fall down
Be killed
You just walk in
They say which one
Would you like
You pick out the color that represents you
From the four colors they offer
You buy the extras dodads
The more dodads the better
You take three of them
Because you can
And with having 3 of them
You feel more secure
Yes you buy the insurance
In case anything happens
And yes some of the extra dodads
Are on sale
There are always extra dodads on sale

You walk out with the sense of you scored
This is when you are robbed
The thieves know
This is where people come out with the goods

The robbers here are more sophisticated
They aren't the ones who bash your head in

That would create fear
People would stop coming here
No they just make it clear
You want to hand over your new purchases
They only take what is covered by the insurance
They let you keep the added dodads
They have empathy

Then you go back in and claim your new items
Since you took out the insurance
Of course
There is a processing fee

We don't seem to interact
With those who really profit
From all the sales
insurances money
Processing fees
Creating underground economies
Making slaves of all of us

Yes they are evil
Some say
Send them to countries where they chop off their heads
While audiences watch
Some are shocked by the violence
They feel
Prison for life is more humane
I say put them in a cell
And slowly fill it up with the dodads
As if death by dodads is more PC

The Master

The Master said
For a $100 – We will shine a light in your face
For $500 – your toes will curl
For $1000 – there will be screams of ecstasy
For $5000 – we will have to call in the authorities

I was looking for something different
When I signed up for the workshop
Jesus was just a regular guy
I was looking for miracles

311

There was an experiment
Each pig was given a number
There were 6,000 pigs
They were all put on old war ships
Anchoring out at sea
Two nuclear bombs were exploded
They wanted to see what would happen
All of the pigs died
Except 311
He was the only one to survive
He was put on a farm
Where he mated with many
Had many children
He lived a long life
I am not superstitious
But I do wear a T Shirt
With 311 on it
311

Stanley Was Waving

My aunt Sophie
Was born in Poland
She remembers one day
Walking home with her mother
They did this walk daily
Always passing the neighbor's farm
Stanley was usually in his garden waving

On this particular day
She remembers as they approached
Her mother grabbed her hand
And started pulling her
As if to rush by the farm

She was resisting
For she loved to stop
Stanley would usually share
Something from his garden
She loved his peaches

Her mother kept pulling her
Faster and faster
She remembers being confused
Waving to Stanley
As they passed by
Stanley waving back

When they got to their house
She noticed her mother
Was sweating
Frightened
Fumbling with the keys
Couldn't get the key in the door

After they were in the house
The doors locked
She asked her mother
Why didn't they stop
Her mother said
Stanley died yesterday

I Have Some Questions

I arrived in Belgium
For a juggling convention
I had a book of translations
Of the language I thought
Was spoken in Belgium

As I walked down a street
Checking menus with the book
None of the words matched
Thinking that it was jet lag
I decided
I would go into
The first restaurant I saw

As I entered the restaurant
I was met by
A force
So ominous
I was pushed across the street
Bewildered
I stood looking at the restaurant
I asked
Where do you want me to go?

There was a restaurant
A few buildings down

I walked in
Everything went fine
Ordered food without complication
As I sat eating
I noticed an older woman
A few tables over
Talking to the waitress

Something about her
Kept drawing me to look over

The waitress left
I was finished eating
I asked
So why was I to come here

The woman
Looked over to me
She spoke to me
In several different languages
Finally saying something to me in English

I found myself sitting at her table
I don't remember getting up
She said to me
You understand this is nothing sexual
I nodded
She said
I have some questions for you

She Already Knew

My mother was in the basement
Doing laundry
As she was putting laundry
Into the washing machine
The basement suddenly felt very cold
She felt the coldness behind her
She then felt a weight
As if a body was pressing against her
The weight of this body
Pressed her up against the washing machine
She felt unable to move
She struggled
She finally broke free
In a cold sweat
Feeling weak in the knees
She crawled up the stairs
To our apartment
Closed the door
And locked it

A few moments later
There was a knock at the door
My mother stood looking at the door
Then she heard
The woman from upstairs
On opening the door
The woman explained
Her husband just died
She wanted to let my mother know

My mother
Already knew

Smokers Die Younger

There was a No Smoking sign
That said Smokers die younger

As I looked around the room
Visiting a nursing home
Many hunched over
Drooling
Others just crying out
I noticed
Mr Jones was trying to escape
Trying to aim his wheelchair
Towards the open door
Howard his best friend
Tried to help
By throwing his food to the ground
As a distraction

I saw a pack of cigarettes
Left on the table
By someone from the last shift
I looked back up at the sign
Smokers Die Younger
Saw Mr Jones made it through the door
I have never smoked
I reached for the pack
I decided to light two..

A Love Poem

I am told
To act from a place of love

So this is a love poem
To the congress
The President and Vice President

Each day brings
New laws that makes all of us criminals
The endless executive orders
That take away everything life giving
The poisoning of everything
The crimes of hate
Are the order of the day

I just wanted to tell ya
How much I am in love
With the day
When you will be gone

Emily

Here in Emily Dickinson's bed room
Will I be a better poet
When I leave
Will I have soaked up the muse
I look out the window and see cars
There were no cars when she lived here
I hear a construction truck beeping
As it backs up
Sounds that I imagine she did not hear
As she sat here listening for words to arrive
It is summer
And there are no screens on the windows
It is cool from the air conditioning
Which she did not have
The wood stove that is in here is very clean
Not used anymore
I wonder how much heat it really produced.
There is a white dress
On a form that stands in the room
I am told this is her dress
She was a very small woman
I was told I couldn't bring in a bag
I was allowed to have my computer
Which Emily didn't have

The bed is small
My understanding is she lived alone
She had her family
But there were no lovers
Who shared this room
Supposedly
Yet how are we to know
I am told she used to be
By the open window

To the street and talk to people
The house and grounds are now being
Kept as a museum
The trees are very large
One of the branches is the size of a large tree

Standing next to the dress
Her head may have come up to my shoulder

I realize I know little about her
I was asked as a poet to read
At her museum
And one of the "payments" was that

You get to spend an hour
In her bedroom
I am told people pay
To rent time to be here
I wondered how Emily feels about
All of these people being in her bedroom

I have to admit
I haven't read
Much of Emily
I started reading late in life
Now I read everything I can get my hands on

I was recently honored
Named Beat Poet Laureate
That I was a new generation
Carrying on the tradition

To know that there were those
Before us
Who felt the need to write

Did Emily travel
Was she mostly here at this house
This room
Only meeting those who visited
Or by letters that were written
Waiting weeks months to get a reaction

My computer lets me know
There is no internet
There wasn't any then
As a writer I use
Methods of writing that
Were not even imagined
Many can see my writings
As I post them daily
She hid them

Now many read her

Hearing people
Walking around
I wonder
How it was to have the door closed
Sitting here
Listening to others in the house
But staying here
To write

There weren't the planes
The missiles
The wars fought on horseback
Experiencing the civil war
Black lives matter
Was the fear the same
Is fear fear

How strange
To think that 200 years later
It looks like we may have another civil war
That the world wars now could
Destroy everything and everyone

There was still a vast wildness to explore
Now one goes from one Walmart parking lot
To the next across the country.

Was there pollution
Did anyone talk of Aliens
There being no TV
Radio
No sports team to cheer on
Or be depressed about

Without the cars and planes over head
It must have been quieter standing in the yard
Working in the garden
Having tea
Now there is the constant
Sounds of trucks and cars driving by
Sirens
It is hard to imagine
What would come to one's mind
With all of the noise gone
There is a hum of some
Mechanized machine
The air conditioner
That she did not have to hear
Or not notice because
You are used to it and it blends in
With the noise of the fridge
The phone is not ringing
What the hell would one do with one's time
Sit and listen

Have more time to listen
To oneself
One's doubts
One's longings
Which are probably no different
Than today but less likely to be heard

As I sit here and run my hands through my hair
A hair falls to the floor
I think that her hair must of hit this same floor
Though it was swept up
Not vacuumed up

The lawn is cut short out the window
I wonder how did it get cut then
Were there animals grazing to keep it down
There were no chemicals to put on
to keep down the weeds
Were they thought of as weeds
Or were they picked as herbs

Looking out the window
I do not time travel and see
What it was like
It could be the sound of the cars
The sounds of today
Don't let me go to the sights of yesterday

Would there be more people walking the streets
The sounds of horses
The smell of horses
Would one run down to the coffee shop
Did one go hunting
Instead of going to the super market
Out to the garden
Was there a farmers market

The dress is long
The pictures of women
Are covered with many layers
A women sits on a bench
Outside in short shorts
Tank top sunning herself

She would have been seen as being naked
Did Emily sun herself
Was it only her face that felt the warmth of the sun
Did she go down to the local pond and jump in
With all the clothes that were required
For women to wear
She might have drowned from the weight

Now young interns
Have jobs here
Greeting visitors
Telling little facts
Have they read Emily
Do they care what she said
Do they fancy themselves the next Emily

Did Emily write about the president
Calling him a fascist
Are the concerns of today
The same she had in a different way
Family squabbles
Misunderstandings
Jealousies
Who liked whom more
Did your friends visit recently
Do you feel betrayed by friends
The gossip of the town
Was the gossip about affairs
Children being born
Stealing

Were the concerns more basic
Were you going to survive the winter
How cold it was
Were you going to get sick
The Doctors who made house calls

Did anyone talk of organic food
There were no GMO's
There was no talk of radiation

Does the staff
Make jokes
About the writers who sit here
In her room writing
As they walk around
Doing this and that
Creating a distraction
For those of us
Trying to find Emily
Here in her room
Is she still here
Does she wonder where has she gone
And why is everyone reading her writings
When she wanted them to be burned

How many buy the books
And don't understand
What they are reading
And think it is themselves
That they just aren't deep enough
To understand
Instead there is nothing to understand
I am writing in the hope to understand

Now we are told
These writings are of someone famous
Made famous

Was the faith of most artists
Then as it is now
Dying in poverty
Starved and dejected
No recognition
Other than they have written something
Later being held up
As great artists

My hour is up
They haven't come for me yet
So am I stealing more time here
Do I feel special
What I have learned
Is that I sat down
For an hour
Noticing the distractions
Using Emily as a prompt
And thought about my life

There is a knock at the door
My hour is up
I talk to staff about my thoughts
About the noises and how quiet
It must have been
They inform me that
It is quieter now
Then when she lived here
There was a
Factory across the street
That rang bells all day long
For changing shifts
The sounds of the horse drawn carriages
Was actually pretty loud
With the sound of horseshoes
Hitting the bricks used in the road
It was a main road

With railroad tracks near by
The steam engines were loud
So everything I imagined
Was not based on the actual reality

I guess I was being a writer
And imaging a world
Creating a whole story
Thanks Emily for the story

Hard To Believe

There was a snow storm
As he was driving
Suddenly his car went into a skid
There were poles to hit, other cars
He missed everything
Went down over the side
Into a ditch
When the car finally stopped
He sat back relieved
He had made it without injury
The car didn't seem worse for the wear
But it wasn't going anywhere
And the snow was really coming down
He managed to call his family
Telling them where he was
That he needed to be picked up
Then he tried getting out of the car
Realizing he needed to climb out
Through the window
It was really slippery once he got out
Getting out of the ditch was a struggle
Finally standing up on the side of the road
Feeling victorious
When he is hit by a sliding car and killed

A New Day

It was a dark night
In a city
Where darkness
Hides nothing

Those huddled under bridges
In cardboard boxes
Covering heating grates

Don't need
Webinars
Explaining
The political
Systematic
Methods of oppression

It's obvious
The system doesn't care

A visceral sound track
Of howling alley dogs
Wailing sirens
Down side streets
Blood pumping terror

Are the sirens
Coming for me?

My ancient
Savage relatives
Cry out to me
As I stand
Where they stood

As I
Wait
For that first sign of light
Of a new day

How To Order Pizza Romantically

Violin Music
Like in the moves
Violin players standing
Around the table
A romantic dinner
As the lovers gaze into each other's eyes

Actually there were no violin players
You could put a quarter in the machine
A speaker at the table
Want to be lovers
Came here after the bars closed
It was rumored the owner made all his money
From all those quarters
Keeping the violin music going

We are staring into each others eyes
While the fake violin music is playing
Wondering who was going to give in
Were we getting the pizza
With the anchovies and artichokes
Or were we getting
Fresh mozzarella and roasted tomatoes

This doesn't happen in the movies
Everything just flows
Lovers wanting the same thing
Not stuck with
Each of us wanted something different

This decision
Was blocking out the violin music

This was not looking good

For posing the question
Will we be lovers tonight?

There really should be a more romantic
Way of ordering a pizza we both want

So he said
You know anchovies and artichokes give me gas
Lets go with your favorite pizza
I want you to have what you want
She contained herself from bursting out laughing
For she saw this as a lame attempt at being romantic
She hated getting gifts
With the obvious hopes
Of making love
She hated that there wasn't going to be a fight
Since she was into make up sex
Now that it was clear there would be no sex
She decided to fight anyway
Asking him how he could be so tasteless
To destroy a pizza with anchovies and artichokes

The fight raged
Until the waiter arrived
They ordered separate dishes
That they were disappointed with

On arriving home she went to bed
Saying she had a headache
He stayed up late on his computer
Researching how to make pizza ordering
More romantic
Which led him to finding some site
Where he could watch naked women
Making pizza with Anchovies and artichokes
Feeling vindicated

Motheer Truckers

On this mother's day
I'd like to call out the Mother Truckers
They know who they are
They give Mothers who drive trucks
A bad name
Mother Truckers
Will drive right over you
Mothers who drive Trucks
Deliver comfort and safety
Mother Truckers
Believe they are the only ones who count
Where Mothers who drive trucks
Have everyone pile in

Mother Truckers
Seem to have a death wish
For they never seem to stop
Unless they are stopped
For good

Mothers who drive trucks
Brings everyone together
Make sure everyone is heard
And the ones who aren't Mother Truckers
Will help take care of everyone

If you are out on the road
A tip of the hat
When you see a mother
Driving a truck
But be careful
If you run into
One of those
Mother Truckers

Parting Words at the Funeral

People stepped forward and said

He was a drunken slob
He beat his wife and abandoned his kids
He made my life Hell
I am glad he's dead

He was my older brother
He beat the shit out of me
He dominated my life
Taking anything he wanted
I thought of killing him several times
I am glad he's dead

Everyone at the church
Thought he was a saint
He played the organ every Sunday
When we came home from church
He beat me and my sister
I am tired of the lies
I am glad he's dead

He lied
He stole
He cheated
He was tormented
He was never the same after the war
He wanted it all to just be over
May he rest in peace
I am glad he's dead

She said
She never wanted children
We stopped her

From doing everything she wanted to do
She beat us
She pushed us away
Told us how much she hated us
We all wanted to be free of her
I am glad she's dead

He was my older brother
Everyone said I was lucky
To have an older brother
After years of abuse
Being raped by him
I am really glad he's dead

Thank you all for coming here today
We are sorry to not have time to hear from all of you
If you could tell the people towards the back
We are out of the allotted time
To show your respect for the dead
Besides the food is getting cold
And people want the bar
To open

If I may speak for all of you in closing
We all share feelings
Of relief and joy
We are all really, really glad
They are dead
May we all find a way to rest in peace

Austin Cafe

The waitress said
There are no substitutes to the menu
I said I don't want a substitute
I want the real thing

I picked something from the menu
The waitress asks
What do you want with that
I asked when she gets off work
She said
From what you ordered
I may be too spicy for you
I said I like spicy
She said I'll bring you some cayenne
She winked and says
Lets see how you handle that first..

A Teachable Moment

I walked into this cafe
They said we don't serve people like you
I thought
Ok
This is going to be a teachable moment
I wasn't planning on going to the hospital
I had some other plans
I was told
They don't like my kind
Here I thought I was being kind
When I picked up the table
I had thought of throwing it
Through the front window
But then thought that would be a drag
For those sitting at the window
So instead I threw it at the guy
Coming at me with the baseball bat
Defending myself
Enraged them even more

I had heard their coffee sucked
I had thought suckie coffee
Over no coffee
Was a better choice
This turned out to be a teachable moment
I now have a different perspective
It's ok to go without coffee

Things Change

Getting directions
A map on a phone
Shows the names of the businesses
Highlights places of interest
Old Salty's was here
Where they kept the glasses in the freezer
People traveled from afar
To get those cold drinks
Now just a memory
Replaced by
Gas for less
Where there is nothing special
Gas
Junk food
If you are lucky
There are clean bathrooms

Being Helpful

You are a complete loser
Scum ranks higher
A pathetic human being
You are the bottom of the foodchain

I
always
appreciate
constructive
criticism

Push The Button

Parking Garage
I pulled up to the gate
The usual routine
You push a button
Take a ticket
I am pushing the button
No ticket appears
See other buttons
I am pushing those buttons
No ticket appears
I am pushing all of them at once
No ticket appears
I am trying to read the 4 easy instructions
Which tell me to push the button
I am pushing the button and yelling
Suddenly
A voice
Out of the speaker
Hi I am Charlie
Do you need some help
I say Hi Charlie
I am having one of those day
Where I am pushing buttons
Things are supposed to be happening
And nothing is happening
I push the button one more time
So Charlie knows I know where the button is
And I can push it
And there is no ticket showing up
I say see I push the button
Nothing happens
Charlie says that's my life in a nut shell
I say to Charlie
I am sorry to hear that

Anything I can do

Thanks for asking
No one ever asks how I am doing

Horns start blowing behind me
People are getting restless
I stick my head out the window
And yell back
I am trying to give Charlie some love here

People are in a hurry
They want to park their cars
And get on with what they are doing
Charlie hears the honking
Tells me here take the ticket
That suddenly appears
I say thanks Charlie
I hope you are feeling better
I wish I could do something
Bring you some joy
Charlie says
I'm going to have my fun
With that honker behind you

They'll be pushing buttons
Screaming
Yelling
I need a ticket
I'll ask
Did you push the button
You need to push the button
Your ticket will appear
Thank You for using Serenity Acres Parking Garage
Push the button if you need further help
Push the button
Push the button

Napping Clothes

I would like to offer to everyone
something from the old country
that my grandmother's grandmother
grandmother used
Napping Clothes

Hardly used any more
you can get them in a six pack
in six beautiful colors
from me

How do they work
is a mystery
defies scientific investigation

A participant holds
one of the small clothes
while laying down
thinking of grandma's love
if grandma was a sonofabitch
you think of aunt Sofie
and before you know it
you are sound asleep

The secert grandma said
was they gave you permission
to take a nap

They are on sale now
for only 29.99
on ebay for $7.99

Support sustainable products
These are made from organic hemp

grown by farmers feeding their families
Sewed by grandmothers sewing clubs
raising lunch money
for their grandkids

Message me
and I'll meet you in the costco parking lot
have correct change
and I'll drive by
and hand you the paper bag

Soon you will be enjoying a nap

Secret Agent

7573247DB65

I am on a mission

You are probably wondering what it is

It was a secret to me for many years

I learned I was to investigate myself

I found out I was one of the many main characters

In this story

I have meet many other main characters
Some are boring
I enjoy the crazy ones

All our stories have some things in common

We were all looking for clues

I am asked

What did you find while investigating yourself
Are you a super hero
Did you find a cape in the closet

Some fear the ending of this story

I am hoping for the best

I continue to search for clues

I search inside and out
I'd like to tell you I've figured it out

Then we could wrap this story up

Many don't want to hear
That there are many different endings
The story keeps going

With us or without us

Accepting we are going to lose all the main characters

I try to tell myself to remain calm
As I look into the mirror
757654B65B

Did I get those numbers wrong
Did I just create a new identity
We all know what that means
When you start changing
That changes the whole story
Many worry
That's the beginning of the end

Reviews

Randy Barnes - Outrider Book Gallery owner, has been collecting the best of modern literature and poetry for 45 years. National Beat Poetry Foundation, Inc Historian

Reading Paul Richmond's new book one gets the feeling that somewhere in Ohio it's raining french fries and all the grocery stores are out of ketchup. Or the recent scientific discovery that the mysterious sound emanating from space that resembles a bell ringing is, in fact, the song of the Earth rotating on its axis which, of course, has nothing to do with Richmond's bells, hiding in the weeds and in junk store boxes while one ponders their retail value on ebay. Whether it be a mongrel dog threatening to eat your leg or an atheist Sunday school teacher makes little difference in the Land of Silence. And further, we are informed that we who are victims (of whatever brand) are the creators of more victims. Yes, the goon squads run with impunity and there's no star far enough to escape the drunken bartender swindling dinero from his thirsty clientele. We're also told that artists are fucked and walls make us all refugees and there's this crazed motherfucker sick with war trying to sell rocks, yes, you heard me, Rocks, for a meager living. Then the old folks home where one's name isn't one's name and the true meaning to one's life becomes state sanctioned sedation.

Need I continue? We live in a very strange and awkward world. There's a killer virus on the loose. Nobody has a job. The national economy is imploding. Fascism is on the rise. But take heart people. There's a way out of this mess, as Ed Dorn reminded us years ago, "Entrapment is this society's sole activity....and only laughter can blow it all to rags." Well, Richmond has a lifetime pass to ride that train. Sober, wry, understated humor is his trademark. And, one more thing. This is a terrific book. Buy it. Read it. Tell your friends, your relatives, and every stranger you meet on the street. Take it from one who knows. I have nothing further to say.

Debbie Tosun Kilday
Owner/CEO National Beat Poetry Foundation,
Inc. and its festivals.

Paul Richmond is a highly respected multi-talented artist, known throughout the US and the world. His writing style touches upon subjects affecting the state of the world we live in. His stories bring our minds back to our childhoods, and make us think about the future. Paul uses his voice and knowledge to defend the natural environment and our right to hold those trying to destroy it, accountable. His hard work has earned him many friends and many titles, including his current role as the US National Beat Poet Laureate (2019-2020) and past title as Massachusetts Beat Poet Laureate (2017-2019). I am honored to know such a talented artist and be a part of the many cultural programs and festivals he creates for spoken word artists, writers, and musicians.

Aprilia Zank, PhD, Beat Poet Laureate, Munich, Germany (Lifetime)

The Winning Deixis – Critical remarks on Paul Richmond's poetry book, *The 24 Hour Store Was Closed*

In his new collection of poems, Paul Richmond takes the reader on an amazing journey through a kaleidoscopic world that ranges from the plain quotidian to the startling bizarre or even para-normal. Like in a modern Decameron, he seems to be driven by the urge to impart and process his, partly traumatic, experiences in order to free himself of their burden. As he declared in a poem, I learnt I was to investigate myself.

In many of his poems, what starts as trivial dailiness evolves into a nightmarish reality with bullying, beating and explosions, or even into a hyper-reality, in which dead people turn up in the most unlikely situations. Paul's poetry is a quest and a report at the same time. Highly cinematic, it 'happens' in front of our eyes and draws us into the happening, whether present or past. With him, we also learn to investigate ourselves, since we discover we have been 'there' as well in the one or the other situation.

One of the main features of Paul's poetic work is its deictic quality, the here, the now and the I/we that make or watch the game. As such, it is perfectly suitable for stage performance. It is the deixis of a seemingly normal reality, but fragile and under threat to be disturbed at any time by either 'the men in uniforms', or the nuclear menace, or the ghosts of the past, or the many other evils lurking everywhere. Turning into an outcast can happen easily and with no obvious reason. Because, like the the veterans in his poems, Paul, too, has a sense that something is wrong. And with his keen sense of the wrong, he

daringly addresses many aspects:
Genocide home and abroad
Slavery
Crushing workers rights
Women rights
Our moral compass of racism
The environmental destruction

Paul's militant voice is vehement and straightforward, but the verbal register of his poetry as a whole is highly nuanced and ranges from the daily trivial tone to witty humorous spontaneity, or skilful sophistication. His poetry challenges the reader precisely through its great diversity in both topics and stylistic devices. When you read his verse, you travel in space and in time, and look forward to the next poem for further thrill and revelation.

Bio

Paul Richmond was awarded Beat Poet Laureate of Massachusetts for 2017 to 2019. Then awarded U S National Beat Poet Laureate for 2019 - 2020 and New Generation Beat Poet Laureate (2022-Lifetime) By the National Beat Poetry Foundation.

Paul's is best described as political, deadpan and wryly humorous delivered in his own style.

He has been called, Assassin of Apathy – power of words / humor - on the unthinkable, the unsolvable, to analyze to digest, to give birth, to creativity and hope

Has performed nationally and internationally; The Austin International Poetry Festival, in Austin TX, in 2011, 2014, 2017, and in 2018 as a featured Poet. A featured poets at Gödör Klubban at the Jazzköltexzeti est in Budapest, Hungary. A featured poet at Beat Festival Stockholm, Sweden. In 2018 performed 12 shows at the Edinburgh Fringe Festival, in Scotland. The Massachusetts Poetry Festival in a featured anthology. Featured Poet at West End Poetry Festival NC. A featured poets in the movie "Trash" by Bucky Jones, all the "dialog" was poetry. Featured Poet 2017, 2018, 2019 at the National Beat Poetry Festival, 2020 Performed in Senegal, Africa with the Senegal – American project.

Published seven books, in many journals, magazines, anthologies and poetry collections. Produces the "Great Falls Word Festival," a mutiple day festival in it's 10th year, the "Word Stage," at the North Quabbin Garlic & Arts Festival, Greenfield Third Tuesday and other events.

Made in the USA
Middletown, DE
26 September 2023

39305729R00064